the UNDENIABLE FAVOR *of* GOD

the

UNDENIABLE
FAVOR

of

GOD

Achieving My Present
by Walking in the
Light of God's Love

ELIZABETH JEAN BRUCE, PH.D.

NEW YORK

NASHVILLE MELBOURNE

the UNDENIABLE FAVOR *of* GOD
Achieving My Present by Walking in the Light of God's Love

Published in New York, New York, by Morgan James Publishing. Morgan James and The Entrepreneurial Publisher are trademarks of Morgan James, LLC. www.MorganJamesPublishing.com

The Morgan James Speakers Group can bring authors to your live event. For more information or to book an event visit The Morgan James Speakers Group at www.TheMorganJamesSpeakersGroup.com.

Shelfie

A **free** eBook edition is available with the purchase of this print book.

CLEARLY PRINT YOUR NAME ABOVE IN UPPER CASE

Instructions to claim your free eBook edition:
1. Download the Shelfie app for Android or iOS
2. Write your name in **UPPER CASE** above
3. Use the Shelfie app to submit a photo
4. Download your eBook to any device

ISBN 978-1-68350-120-6 paperback
ISBN 978-1-68350-122-0 eBook
ISBN 978-1-68350-121-3 hardcover
Library of Congress Control Number:
2016909269

Cover Design by:
Rachel Lopez
www.r2cdesign.com

Interior Design by:
Bonnie Bushman
The Whole Caboodle Graphic Design

Morgan James The Entrepreneurial Publisher™

Builds

with...

Habitat for Humanity®
Peninsula and Greater Williamsburg

In an effort to support local communities, raise awareness and funds, Morgan James Publishing donates a percentage of all book sales for the life of each book to Habitat for Humanity Peninsula and Greater Williamsburg.

Get involved today! Visit
www.MorganJamesBuilds.com

For

Mom
Dad
Johnny
Alice

TABLE OF CONTENTS

Acknowledgements

I would like to thank Michael Ebeling of The Ebeling Agency, for his thoughtful review of my book proposal, and for introducing my book to David Hancock of Morgan James Publishing

I would like to thank Terry Whalin, Acquisitions Editor of Morgan James Publishing, for reviewing my book proposal and accepting my work to submit for publishing at Morgan James Publishing. I would like to thank Terry Whalin for his encouragement and help in the beginning of my publication process.

I would like to thank Kim Spano, Author Relations for Morgan James Publishing

I would like to thank Cindy Sauer, Vice President of Operations for Morgan James Publishing

I would like to thank Eric T. Schroeder for editing my book.

I would like to thank Tiffany Gibson, Managing Editor of Morgan James Publishing, for her help with the final editing details and design of my book.

I would like to thank Jim Howard, Publishing Director for Morgan James Publishing

I would like to thank David Hancock, Founder of Morgan James Publishing

WHAT IN THE WORLD AM I DOING?

*Discovering and Beginning
the Journey toward My Goal*

Childlike Faith

ince I was a child, I could feel the presence of God. I was born into a family who loved God and raised me to know my Creator for myself. I developed a strong belief in and spiritual connection with God very early in life. I remember my first serious conviction regarding the destiny of my soul was around the age of five. I knew I wanted to be saved and make it into

Heaven, but I was not absolutely sure about my present status with God. I was very concerned. I pleaded to God within myself, "Please save me and help me make it into Heaven." One day, while riding in the car with my parents, I asked them, "How can I know I'm going to Heaven?" I felt a great sense of relief when my parents responded to me. They said all I had to do was let God know that I wanted to go to Heaven and that if I asked the Lord to save me, He already had. I could be assured I was going to Heaven. That was a wonderful day for me. I felt much lighter and more carefree. I was very happy and knew from that day forward that I was saved and going to Heaven someday; I have been looking forward to it ever since. Eventually, during later years in elementary school, I did remind the Lord that I still wanted to go to Heaven. I asked Him to do whatever it takes to help me make it in to Heaven.

My relationship with God continued to flourish during my childhood and at age five, I experienced an awesome miracle. I had been born with an itchy round rash on the back of my neck. In hindsight, I suspect it may have been eczema. My parents made many attempts to make the rash go away, including ointments, creams, and doctor visits, but the rash was persistent and uncomfortable. One night, while sleeping alone in my room, I felt a hand on my neck touching the rash.

The hand came from the direction of the wall that my bed was positioned against. It was a supernatural hand. It was a holy hand with a calm, gentle, and precise touch. I knew instantly that I was being healed. I was not afraid or startled. I looked around my room to see if anyone was present, but I didn't see anyone. I went right back to sleep. The next morning, I told my mother, "Someone touched my neck last night." I described the events of the previous evening. When my mother examined my neck, she said, "It's gone!" My rash was completely gone and the skin where it used to be was smooth and flawless! Our family was so happy and excited for that wonderful miracle that God gave me. I have never forgotten that healing touch. For years to come, whenever I had a chance, I would tell anyone who would listen about my healing touch from God. Each time I told the story, my eyes would well up with tears. I remember describing my experience to peers at school. I would often get blank stares, like they were not sure whether to believe me or not, but I continued to share my testimony. I would testify to people at church and extended family members as well. My mother still has a tape recording of me giving testimony to her and my aunt. After I shared my testimony, I said, "He touched me. He really did!" My aunt responded, "He did?" I replied, "He did!" My mother began singing, "He touched me, and made me whole."

Early School Years

My years in school were relatively pleasant. I was never famous or popular, but I always had a few close friends who helped make school enjoyable. Two friends were very close and both friends remained in contact years after elementary school. I was very happy for each of them when they got married and had children.

I was fortunate that the Lord blessed me to do well academically. My mother used to frequently tell a story about a time when she and my father visited my school for teacher-parent night. I was in the third or fourth grade at the time. My mother said that my teacher spent quite a bit of time focusing on my success in class and sharing it with the parent gathering while my father kept dosing off. I was glad to hear that my teacher thought so well of me and I thought it was funny that my father kept dosing off during parent-teacher night.

My first school years, kindergarten through second grade, were at Russ School, in Hayward, California, and Murray School, in Dublin, California. During these first years of school, my favorite part of the day was eating breakfast at home. I always felt warm and cozy while enjoying my first meal before going out into the big wide world. I had a very nice kindergarten teacher who was very supportive of me and communicated with my family frequently. She also was my brother's teacher when he started school. I had begun telling peers at recess about my miracle touch. Issues became a bit more debatable as they related to my witnessing. One day, I shared my testimony to my peers, as usual. Later, during the end of recess as we were all lined up to go inside, the line was near a square sand box. A girl came up to me, rolling her eyes, and made the statement, "There is no God." Then she pushed me to the ground into the sand box. My teacher talked to my parents, explaining what had happened. When my parents learned that I was witnessing at school, they were proud of me. They would say that I was a true witness, even at school.

We moved to Dublin, California when I was in the first grade. At this time, my peers were slightly ahead of me because I transferred schools mid-semester. The class was learning how to count from 0 through 100. I remember feeling really lost, because I could not do what the other kids in class were able to do. I came home and told my mother what was going on. My mother began teaching me to count to 100 at home. I enjoyed learning from my mother at home. Learning to count with my mother felt easy and comfortable. Eventually, I was able to count and do everything my peers could do in class. I felt so much better!

God continued to reveal his love and presence with me throughout my academic endeavors. Our family moved to Phoenix, Arizona, where I began the third grade at Cordova Elementary School. As time went by, I adjusted to my new environment, did well in my school work, and made really good friends. Our neighbors were very friendly and, one Christmas season, our family was showered with love when several families in our neighborhood gave us nice furniture, a Christmas tree, food, and gifts for Christmas. This beautiful gesture came at a time when we needed it, because our furniture was still in storage and we did not have furniture for our home. That was a really nice Christmas!

During the third and fourth grades, I was a member of the Brownies and the Girl Scouts. We met weekly and participated in fun recreational activities. One of my favorite elementary school experiences was writing a play for a class assignment. The play had to be a twist on an already popular children's story. I wrote my play based on the three little pigs. Our class was divided into sections to memorize each other's scripts and to act them out in front of the class. When my group performed the play that I wrote, the class enjoyed it. My teacher later pulled me aside and told me I had a talent for writing plays. The response I received from my teacher and peers was very pleasant and unexpected.

I started to enjoy school more when I began to make close friends. This was around the fourth grade. At that time, I made honor roll for the first time. I still have that honor roll award. I saved it with all of the awards I have earned over the years. My awards are reminders for me of how far God has brought me. He continues to bless me with manifestations of his presence with me and his favor of me.

The Benefit of a Remedial Math Class

There was a brief moment, during my elementary school years, when I felt embarrassed of my academic ability. During the fifth grade, the school gave an academic assessment placement exam to students to see where we stood in several academic domains. The teacher announced there was a special math class for students who did not achieve a high score on the math portion of the exam. The special math class was called "Title I." The teacher announced my name among those who would have to take the Title I class. I was taken off guard to hear that I needed a remedial course. I remember trying to hold back my tears. Someone asked, "Are you crying?" I responded, "Something's in my eye."

Once I got settled into the Title I math class, I began to enjoy it. I think it was one of the best things that happened to me during elementary school. I became a whiz at multiplication!

Learning my multiplication tables made it easier for me to do well in other areas of math, like Algebra. I continued earning honor roll awards, which over the years included iron-on patches, pens, plaques, and trophies. In the sixth grade, I must have been known to do well in my work, because a few male classmates talked me into doing their homework. Our teacher at that time caught on and let us all know she was aware of what had transpired. After that, I did not receive further requests to complete my peers' homework assignments.

When I was to start the seventh grade, our family moved to a new home outside of the school district where we were students. My parents did not want to take me and my siblings out of our current school, so they received permission for us to continue at our present school. I continued at Cordova through the eighth grade and my siblings continued at Cordova until they started junior high school. They eventually attended stand-alone junior high schools in our home school district.

Once I graduated from Cordova, I attended West High School. This school had an ethnically diverse population and I knew quite a few students there who attended the same church as my family. My experience at West High was quite an adventure. I especially enjoyed taking a Spanish class with friendly peers and a nice teacher with a sense of humor.

A Class for the Gifted

At West High, I took a placement exam and tested as gifted in English. I was given the opportunity to join an after-school class for gifted students. We conducted our own research projects, went on field trips, and discussed interesting topics. I enjoyed it. One memory that stands out for me is our field trip to see the movie, "Gandhi." I didn't know the story before and I became more aware of another important issue in the world. I learned about the caste system in India and how a peaceful man protested it. The subject "Gandhi" inspired me.

During my gifted class, I designed a research project. I received input from many students at my high school who completed a survey that I developed about television-watching habits. I was very excited about my work and interested in my peers' input. Unfortunately, at this time, I learned that our family would be moving to a different city. I became despondent. I did not know what to do and I did not really know how to say goodbye to my teachers and classmates. I regret that one day I threw all of the surveys that my peers had completed into a trash bin in the school hallway. I still feel bad when I think about that. I wish I had kept my surveys and been able to review the responses later.

An Unexpected Turn of Events

I enjoyed friendship and fun while I attended West High, but not without a few occasions of danger. One specific incident was a day I was wearing a pair of my mother's boots that my father brought her from a business trip in New York. When I decided to wear my Mom's boots, I had no idea that later in the day I would be sinking the heels of my mother's brand new boots into 2-inch-deep mud, running away from a stranger. The boots were mid-height with three inch heels. It had been rainy for a few days prior, so some areas of the ground were deep with mud. On this day, a friend and I decided to walk off-campus for lunch. My friend told me about recent run-ins she had with a pimp and that he continued to bother her. We were walking behind the school through an alley to a street where other students were walking. Suddenly, at the end of the alley, someone pulled up in a long vintage maroon car and says, "Hey!" Immediately my friend exclaims, "That's him!" She grabbed my arm, and we turned back around to run as fast as we could toward our school. I was trying to run fast in my mother's high heel boots through a muddy alley. I could not believe this was happening! I remember hiding in a corner by a wooden fence, hoping the man in the car had decided to leave us alone. Finally, when we saw the man was gone, we ran the rest of the way back to our school campus. My friend and I had made it safely back to school. I thought to myself, "I will never go off campus for lunch again!" I eventually resumed occasional walks to lunch off campus, but I always used the main side walk with the rest of the pedestrian traffic.

A Change in High School

When I was a sophomore in high school, our family moved to Tucson, Arizona where I attended Saguaro High. Life in Tucson was interesting. In school I was able to make really close friends with whom I ate lunch and enjoyed free time. My first acquaintances were from the Black Culture Club. A group of girls from the club introduced themselves to me and welcomed me to join them. During lunch, we would watch boys play basketball. I enjoyed meeting the girls, but I was pretty shy and did not quite know what to say, so I was quiet much of the time. Eventually, the girls did not come around anymore.

I met another friend with whom I became very close. She introduced me to her group of friends who were also very nice. At lunch time they enjoyed following boys that they liked around campus. My friend invited us to party celebrations and family gatherings at her home. Everyone was very friendly and enjoyed these times together in celebration. It was always fun to be around them. My friend's family heritage was Irish and Spanish. One time, she invited me to a St. Patrick's Day celebration. The adults were looking through the glass doors and pointing to Leprechauns in the back yard and telling the children, "See there's a Leprechaun." We stayed in touch for years after high school, and when she got married, she sent me family pictures before our communication ended.

During my sophomore year at Saguaro High, I worked in the administration office as part of my school schedule. In debate class, we were given assignments to prepare debates for or against specific topics. I remember a debate I participated in, during which I argued for gun control. This experience helped me understand how there could be valid arguments for multiple perspectives of political issues. I found classes at Saguaro to be interesting as well as educational.

From Arizona to California
Our family moved to Vallejo, California when I was a junior in high school. The high school I attended in Vallejo was ethnically diverse and many students who attended went to the same church as our family. When we first moved to Vallejo, friends of my parents picked us up from the San Francisco Airport. The Democratic National Convention was in session and the airport and city were bustling with energy. We spent the evening at our family friends' home and later reserved a room at a local motel, where we stayed until we

found our own place to live. We eventually rented a home from our friends. We would stay there during our three years in Vallejo.

Hogan High

There were two major high schools in Vallejo: Vallejo High and Hogan High. These schools were friendly rivals. Homecoming and other football games were big events. Even though I never attended homecoming or a football game, I enjoyed the excitement and feeling of anticipation in the environment during these times. I attended Hogan High. I found my classes at Hogan to be interesting and I did well in them. I remember two classes in particular: social studies and health class. I remember once in my social studies class, the instructor had asked a question in class and I had completed the class reading assignment the night before. There was a quiet pause in the class and no one would answer the question. I slowly raised my hand, and when the instructor called on me, I gave my answer. The instructor confirmed that my answer was correct. I felt really scholarly that day, having read and remembered pertinent information and demonstrated knowledge of my homework topic.

In my social studies class, I gained more experience considering various perspectives on political issues. We were instructed to write a one page summary of the good qualities of Ronald Reagan, President of the United States, and leave it on our desks at the end of class on the due date. The instruction seemed to come out of nowhere. I was not yet old enough to vote, but in most cases, I would have voted Democrat. Since being old enough to vote, I have always been a registered Democrat. There have been a very few times when I voted Republican, like when I was disappointed that Jesse Jackson was not chosen as the 1988 running mate for the Democratic presidential candidate. I was determined to complete my homework assignment with objective accuracy and competency. I did some serious research and gathered factual information and looked at positive qualities that I could notice in the President. I was pleasantly surprised to find several positive attributes of the current President. One attribute that I included in my paper was the establishment of Dr. Martin Luther King, Jr.'s birthday as a national federal holiday. I remember completing my paper and being happy that I was able to complete my assignment as instructed, with no reservations about anything that I had written.

I also enjoyed my health class. The instructor was very friendly and knowledgeable about health issues. He answered many pertinent inquiries of my class peers, informatively and without being daunted. I enjoyed learning in the social atmosphere in my health class at Hogan. One day we saw a movie about a woman giving birth. We saw the whole process and I remember that, for me, it took some of the mystery out of what was involved in giving birth. In addition to learning about child birth, we also learned about safe birth control methods. We were shown various contraceptives and how they worked. I thought it was interesting seeing these items up close and learning how they worked. Some of them I had not heard of before. This experience educated me more about options available for couples who are not ready to become pregnant.

At Hogan, I had a few close friends with whom I ate lunch frequently, but I do remember times when I ate lunch alone, either in the cafeteria, in a class room, or outside. I was still quite shy and I had discussed with my mother that I was seriously considering a career where I would not have to interact with people very much. (Who would have thought that I would end up continuing my education to become a psychologist?) At this time, I thought a career in computer technology or computer repair would be a good way to avoid social situations. I had even spoken with my high school counselor and informed her that I would like to work in the computer technology field; however, the wheels in my mind were still turning.

A Defining Moment

One day I realized that I wanted to have a career where I could help people more directly. I knew I did not want to be a physician; I would not be able to handle the intricacies involved in healing the human body. One night when I was a high school junior, I was watching 20/20 with my mother. That night one of the featured guests was a child psychologist. During the interview, the child psychologist was sitting down and around him were a group of young people he had been working with. The young people shared how they were helped by the psychologist in their lives. I said to my mother, "That's what I can do!" My mother encouraged me and agreed that I could do it. From then on, I was determined to become a psychologist, emphasizing work with young people.

I graduated high school in 1986 and focused my academic career on completing the requirements for the field of psychology. My first post-secondary school was Solano Community College, in Suisun, California. I took my psychology introduction course at a satellite in Vallejo at the city library which was located near a marina. I made friends with a classmate at my satellite class, which made the class more enjoyable. For the rest of my classes I went to campus by city bus and a shuttle that picked students up at the bus depot in Vallejo. I enjoyed the commute. The shuttles were generally spacious and quiet with several other students who were commuting. Sometimes there were more students on the shuttle than at other times. Additional courses I took at Solano Community College included a computer writing course and an English literature course. I also took a Spanish course. I enjoyed my Spanish course, due to the instructor and a few classmates. The instructor encouraged me to continue to a more advanced course in Spanish, but I lacked confidence and did not pursue further advancement, though it felt very nice that he considered me a good candidate.

I made a close friend on campus at Solano Community College. We kept each other company during free times, lunch time, time between classes, and while waiting to take the shuttle home from campus. She would bring Milano cookies to share and tell me funny stories about her social life. Once she told me a story about the new wives of some formerly close platonic male friends. The wives would ask her to stop calling and writing their husbands. One day, my friend said that she told one of the wives that she just wanted to remain friends. She said that the wife responded, "Liar!" I really enjoyed laughing with my friend during our time together. We stayed in contact for a few years after junior college, writing letters and sending cards.

When our family moved from Vallejo to San Jose, I attended San Jose City College, where I eventually earned my Associate of Arts degree. I enrolled in classes in anthropology, music, and psychology. I don't remember making any close female friends during my time at San Jose City College, but I did make several male friends, with whom I studied for classes and enjoyed visiting outdoor school festivals.

Practice in Navigating Academic Training at a University

After graduating from San Jose City College, I attended a state university for approximately one year. My courses included psychology, statistics, and English. In addition to starting at a large university, I was also adjusting to moving with my family into another home. I was struggling somewhat in my courses and my grades were showing it. In particular, I remember being extremely stressed over some difficulty I was having understanding the material in my statistics class. I was so preoccupied with trying to understand the content of the statistics curriculum that I continued trying to figure it out during an earthquake. One day, I was sitting in my room on my bed, trying to complete statistics homework. Suddenly my bed lifted off of the ground and began swaying from side to side and my VCR was vibrating toward the edge of my dresser. In the middle of all of this, I actually kept trying to study! I could feel the ground roll like waves under my bed and I could see things shaking all around me and I was worried about my Statistics class. I finally ran out of my room to see how everyone else was doing. We all gathered in our living room and stayed close together until the earth stopped moving. A few of us stood in the front entrance doorway while looking outside. It was a bright beautiful sunny day, though frightening. Eventually we learned, from news broadcastings on television, a major earthquake occurred, with the epicenter being near the San Francisco/Oakland area. My father was working in San Bruno at that time, so we were glad when he got back home with us! In the following days, there were recurring shock waves that continued to reach San Jose. I remember being on a high level floor at the university library and feeling the floor vibrate. Talk about prayer! I looked around through the windows at the beautiful sunny day and prayed that the shaking would stop. After a few minutes, the ground stopped shaking and I resumed studying.

My grades during my year at the university were not great, but at the time, I thought they would suffice. When I tried to get my official transcripts, school administrators would not release my grades to me, because I had not yet paid my tuition. When I did try to pay my tuition, the school administrators said it was too late and they would not take my money or release my official transcripts. I've learned, since this time, that whenever I try my best and it seems like I'm running into a brick wall, that it is God protecting me from things I am unaware of at that time. Looking back, I see that the school administrators did me a favor. Not only was I able to become acquainted with navigating classes and learning the system of a large university, but I was able to do it free of charge and without having my grade point average be negatively affected.

Earning my Bachelor of Arts

Eventually our family moved to Sacramento, California, where I attended California State University, Sacramento (CSUS). I graduated CSUS in 1994 with a Bachelor of Arts. I majored in psychology and minored in communications. My field work advisors in the Department of Psychology nominated me for two awards. On May 6, 1992, I won the Douglas A. Michell Memorial Scholarship in the Department of Psychology. This came with a $300 reward. On March 1, 1993, I won the Minority Undergraduate Student of Excellence Award from the American Psychological Association. My last semester of college, I was on the Dean's Honor List.

At this time I really enjoyed attending school. I actually looked forward to Mondays after the weekends! I think I enjoyed the feeling of independence. I liked attending orientation, learning the process of registering for classes, choosing my own schedule, being in large classrooms that were like little auditoriums, and going to the new student union building for free time and in the mornings before classes. In order to stay aware of current events, and be able to discuss them in class or with family, friends, and acquaintances, I would usually get to school early in the mornings and watch <u>The Today Show</u> with Bryant Gumbel before going to class. I made a few close friends at CSUS, with whom I sat in class and some who I enjoyed spending time with outside of class. I continued to use the CSUS library a few years after graduating. I had library privileges as an alumnus. Library privileges came in handy during graduate school when I was doing research while at home in Sacramento.

While I attended CSUS, my field work advisors treated me like family. I had two main advisors. One was the senior advisor and the other was mentored by him while she mentored me. I enjoyed talking to and working with both of them. Had they not informed me of and encouraged me, I would not have applied for the awards I won during my time at CSUS. As part of my application for the Douglas A. Michell Memorial Scholarship, I was required to write a brief paper discussing my dreams for the future. I knew what my dreams were, but I was a little shy about exposing them. What if my dreams never came true? While I was sitting in front of my paper thinking about my dreams, something told me, "Write it out! Don't be ashamed." I immediately began writing with determination that I would pursue my goals without fear or timidity. I wrote about my dream of becoming a psychologist to provide help and guidance for emotionally disturbed youth.

My life experience as an African American has influenced my interest in learning about how diverse ethnic groups can live among each other in harmony, as well as how resiliency against negative life circumstances, such as economic disadvantage and racial bias, can be developed in individuals at an early age. During my time at CSUS, I completed my field work at Mac Elementary School, located in an ethnically-diverse community in Sacramento. As I observed graduate students who were working and conducting research studies there, I learned about conflict resolution and I was also able to sit in on counseling sessions with students.

After my field work at Mac Elementary, I was able to gain field work experience working with children at St. Hope Academy, an after-school program for inner-city students. I enjoyed my volunteer work with the students, providing encouragement, tutoring, and being a positive role model. Sometimes, I had fun conversations with the students. One conversation I had stands out in my mind, because my father and I laughed about it for some time afterwards. One of my younger tutees asked me, "Do you get paid?" When I responded,

"No," she stated matter-of-factly, "When I work here, they're gonna pay me." After my work at St. Hope that day, my father arrived at the academy for our drive home together. When he asked how my day went, I told him about my conversation with the student. He thought that was very funny and thought she had a point. I agreed with my father that the student's statement was humorous and we laughed.

The following year, I was able to work at St. Hope as an employee, teaching Black History in the Summer Enrichment Program. I developed a curriculum and taught the children information I found fascinating and encouraging as an African American. It was fun to share information with the students from ancient history, recent history, and current day accomplishments of Black people in society. My hope is that what children learned has motivated them to achieve great things themselves.

Now What?

When I graduated CSUS, I was in the process of applying to graduate schools. After several applications and no positive responses, I got a little discouraged. Once, my sister went with me to an interview at a school in Pasadena, California. The trip was a nice adventure, even though I was not accepted into the school program. One of the incidents that made that trip memorable was a comic moment with my sister after a disappointing interview. I was interviewed by a panel of staff and I was asked what well-known psychologists inspired me. I mentioned two people who inspired me, one of which was not a psychologist. Suddenly one of the members on the panel responded, rather rudely, "He's not a psychologist." I was taken aback and, though I was able to complete my interview, I don't think that I was able to establish a very good rapport with any of the panel members. I felt distraught when I met my sister in the waiting room. She was reading a book that my mother had loaned her. I sat down next to her in a chair and told her about what had transpired. Utilizing newly discovered concepts she had learned from her reading and reciting the title of the book, my sister encouraged me, "You have to Embrace Your Pain." Immediately, the intensity of my pain decreased and I laughed hysterically, receiving my sister's advice. I asked if I could look through the book she was reading for a few minutes. Through my sister, God almost instantly eradicated all my personal pain associated with the interview. I was really glad to have such help so readily available at the precise time I needed it.

I remember, a few months after my graduation, laying across my bed during the day and wondering what on earth I could do. Just as my mind began to spiral into sadness, the Lord spoke to me and said, "Get up and find a job." I immediately got up from my bed and started thinking about what kind of job I could qualify for that would prepare me further for a career in psychology. I informed my mother and father, who encouraged me. I searched the newspaper for jobs that I would be interested in and found a job that was perfect for me. It was working as a counselor in a group home for adolescent girls. The requirement was a Bachelor's degree – exactly what I had! I was excited to gain further experience that would help me in my goal toward becoming a clinical child psychologist.

During my work at the group home, I learned a lot of important things that helped me mature in my thinking and in my skills working with young people. I gained empathy for young people who had experienced tragic events and were trying to live life as best as they could. As a mentor I was able to develop rapport with the girls and I brought a few girls to church events on my own and attended several church services with the group home as a whole. There were a few times when crisis situations arose, but God helped me be a part of the staff team that remediated these situations. Once during a crisis situation, I was standing by the bed of one of the girls. I began praying. The girl in crisis looked at me and said, while laughing, "Are you praying?" I responded "Yes! I'm praying!" She smiled, and seemed to calm down after that. We kept in touch when she went to another facility for a while, and I sent her gospel music tapes to listen to. I gave several of the girls gospel music tapes, and I looked forward to sharing music with them that was inspiring to me, because I knew it would be uplifting for the girls as well.

I worked at the group home for two years before I finally was accepted into a Ph.D. program. I had saved enough money to apply to more graduate schools. I would be attending the Pacific Graduate School of Psychology, PGSP (now known as Palo Alto University, PAU). When I received the acceptance letter at home, I was so happy that I could not stop jumping up and down. I would stop jumping for a few minutes and then I would start jumping up and down again. I was in the family room and my mother and father were in the kitchen, which is adjacent and open to the family room. I told them the news while I was jumping and they were smiling and happy for me. I could not believe it. I was finally going to graduate school for my Ph.D. in clinical psychology!

MY LIFE DURING GRADUATE SCHOOL

Enjoying an Adventurous Journey

I started graduate school in the fall of 1997. My father and sister attended an evening orientation with me. We did not have a car at that time, so we caught the city bus to the Greyhound station. We rode the Greyhound from Sacramento to San Francisco, a local express bus into a Palo Alto bus depot, and a cab to the school.

A professor (who eventually was a co-chair on my dissertation committee) was providing the orientation lecture in one of the classrooms. PGSP was a small private professional school, located in a relatively quiet residential area. The school comprised two main buildings across the street from and facing each other. One building held faculty offices, classrooms, a library, a student lounge, and a treatment clinic, where students received clinical training and supervision while providing psychotherapy for patients in the community. The building across the street was designed more formally. It contained the financial assistance office, an upstairs platform (where one of my later classes was held), and a conference room where students, faculty, and guests frequently convened for lecture lunches with guest speakers and group meetings.

On orientation night, my father, sister, and I were directed to the classroom where orientation was in progress. We had arrived a little late, but the professor did not make an issue of it. He was polite and courteous, continuing his introduction of the school to the attendees. While I attended the orientation, my father and sister waited for me in the lounge area and met several people. My father later shared with me some interactions he had conversing with others in the lounge while waiting for me. After orientation, my father, sister, and I caught a cab and began our trip back home to Sacramento. I was very excited about being accepted into graduate school and earning my doctorate in clinical psychology.

My first classes at school were held every other day and/or in the afternoons. This made it easier for me to continue living at home with my parents and commute to school by bus. I usually spent the night at a nearby Motel 6 after school if I had to be at school again the next day. I would go home after class if I did not have school the following day. If I had an early morning class, I would spend the night at the motel. I was enjoying my frequent travels and meeting a variety of nice and interesting people during my trips. I remember always being excited about everything and full of anticipation. I enjoyed every aspect of my life: traveling, attending school, utilizing my energy and creativity for completing school assignments, and meeting new people at school and during travels. The journey toward my goal was an adrenaline rush for me. I was never tired. I would come home, do homework, get ready, and begin my commute to Palo Alto again. My trips usually started around midnight, when my parents would take me to the Greyhound station so I could catch the bus to San Francisco. There would be a three or four hour layover in San Francisco before my next bus arrived to go to San Jose. From San Jose I would catch a local city bus into Palo Alto and another city bus to the school.

On nights when I stayed at the Motel 6, I only had to catch one city bus from the motel to school. I discovered this fact after trial and error. Initially, I would wake up very early in the mornings to catch a bus in front of the motel, going the wrong way, back to the downtown bus depot, and catch another bus coming back around to a bus stop only a few blocks away from where I was already staying at the motel. I completed this trip for several weeks. One day, while riding in the car with my parents and family when they were visiting me in Palo Alto, I was proudly explaining my morning commutes by the city bus to school. A family friend, who lived locally, said "The bus stop is right here." She was pointing to a bus stop near the motel where I stayed. Everyone started laughing hysterically when I realized that I had been making a trip around the city just to arrive back at a bus stop that was a few blocks around the corner from my current location. After I was properly oriented, I began walking the five blocks to the bus stop located in front of a small shopping center (where I sometimes ate at restaurants and shopped for clothing, food, and other items) on school mornings. I no longer had to wake up quite as early as I had been to get ready for school.

My brother lived in San Jose, so he would visit me at the motel sometimes when I got out of school in the evenings, bringing my little niece along with him. One day, we were all at home with my parents in Sacramento and we passed by a motel. My niece proclaimed, "There's Aunt Liz's house."

I was really having fun and my life, as busy as it was, was flowing smoothly and I was enjoying the ride. My mother would help me practice for Clinical Interviewing class by allowing me to video tape us role-playing therapy sessions. Usually this occurred at night, just before my parents took me to the Greyhound station. One night I was completing a paper for a class that was due soon. I had my papers scattered in front of the fire place at home, organizing them before getting ready to make my trip back to school. I felt like I was on some kind of high or rush all of the time. It was a good rush, like something exciting and new was about to happen.

Reality Reveals Itself

One day things began to slow down, just a tad bit. I started to have difficulty in my statistics I class. It seemed like a foreign language to me. There were many students in the class and there were frequent study groups which I attended, but I just could not grasp the material. (I found that I study better alone.) I failed my statistics class, which put somewhat of a wrench in my academic schedule, because the class was only offered at specific times of the year. I could not retake it the following quarter, because ideally I was supposed to be attending statistics II class the next quarter. To top it off, I would eventually have to complete a comprehensive exam which included material from both courses.

I was able to take other valuable courses while I waited for my second chance to take statistics I. I took my clinical comprehensive exam and passed on my second attempt. Two quarters later, I was able to enroll in the statistics I class again. You would not believe what happened. I failed the class again. It was at this point when I just very briefly wondered if I would ever be able to get past this hurdle and I thought about giving up. To make matters worse, a school committee voted to have me dis-enrolled from the school!

With the help of my research advisor and my fieldwork advisor, who were a part of an appeal committee, I was able to continue my course work at school and finish working toward my Ph.D. In order to demonstrate my seriousness about finishing successfully, I was asked to write a plan of steps I would take in order to improve my academic standing. My plan included attending a summer school statistics class at my undergraduate alma mater, CSUS, while waiting for the next statistics I class at PGSP, auditing the statistics II class at PGSP in the upcoming quarter, and getting a tutor to help me prepare for my next statistics I class.

Fortunately, the school hired a very helpful tutor for me. He was also a PGSP student. I could not believe how clear the material had become and how easy the course work could be. The work was tedious, but understandable. I had just needed individual help to be able to understand it. After learning how to operate the statistics problems, I actually enjoyed it! After two quarters, I was able to take the statistics I course again. Finally, I passed statistics I with a B-. The next quarter, in statistics II, I received a B- the first time around. Later, I passed my Statistics Comprehensive Exam with an 80%.

In the meantime, during the two-quarter interval before my final statistics I course, I had the opportunity to attend a class at Stanford University. It was a privilege to be able to attend such a prestigious university, even for just one course. I was able to walk around the campus, go to the bookstore, eat in the cafeteria, meet students there, and get a general feeling of how it was to attend Stanford. My class there, Career and Personal Counseling for Culturally Diverse Groups, was a part of a cooperative relationship between PGSP and Stanford. I enjoyed working with the professor of the class and working with my client in the clinic portion of the course. It was a positive experience.

Happy Again

By the time I passed my statistics courses, I had completed most of the other course requirements and had started my field work, earning practicum hours working with children. The hurdle had been overcome, my carefreeness came back, and I was happy again. I remember one of the office administrators commenting to me, "You sure seem very happy. What's going on?" I explained that I was finished with my course work and I did not have to go to classes anymore.

Now I could focus on my dissertation research and my field work, even though I did have an oral exam to prepare for in the near future. My first practicum site, the place where I received training and supervision while working with clients, was at an elementary school in San Jose. I had the privilege of providing therapy to first and second grade students who were experiencing behavioral problems in class. Though they seemed restless at times, these children were, for the most part, pleasant and still seemed to have a youthful hope for life. I enjoyed working with each of my clients and working with their teachers, parents, and the principal of the school. My on-site supervisor and my fieldwork supervisor at school were very pleasant and helpful to work with. Everyone provided positive role modeling and constructive advice and was instrumental in helping me increase my clinical skills. After my practicum work at the elementary school, I received very nice recognition with a presentation of a certificate signed by my on-site supervisor and the school principal. I later received a note from one of my former clients through the practicum student who was now working with her, letting me know that she missed me and her favorite memories of our work together. It was a very nice feeling to know that one of my little clients remembered my work with her in such a positive way.

Fun Adventures

Before my next scheduled practicum site interview, I decided to attend the Summer Olympic Trials in Sacramento. I discovered that the trials would be taking place at CSUS, with opening day being the day I was planning to leave for Burlingame to interview for my next practicum training. I knew attending the Olympic trials in my home city at my alma mater was a once in a lifetime chance and I wanted to take advantage of it. Fortunately, I had time to enjoy a day at the trials and leave for my interview later in the evening. This was another exciting

Me at Olympic trials, California State University, Sacramento, 7/13/00

day for me. Even though I remember being disappointed that one of my favorite male track stars was not there, I had a great time watching the trials anyway. I met really nice people who were sitting near me on the bleachers and we talked about the events. At the event booths, I had a portrait taken of me with an Olympic medal around my neck while standing in front of the American flag. I still have the photo. As the evening progressed and the trials were ending for the day, I headed toward the light rail station with my overnight bag to catch a ride to the Greyhound station downtown, take a bus to San Francisco, and then take an express bus to Burlingame for my interview the next day. I was happy to have had an experience at the Summer Olympic Trials and I was happy to be going to an interview for my next practicum training. I was enjoying it all!

My interview in Burlingame went well and I was accepted into the practicum program. It was at a non-profit child and family clinic. I gained experience working with ages four through adult. I gained skills in group therapy, individual therapy, and family therapy. I enjoyed working with my clients and I met several other practicum students who were pleasant to work with as well as enjoy free time with. I also enjoyed working with my supervisors who were all very friendly and helped me increase my clinical skills. After my practicum was complete, there was a goodbye luncheon for practicum students at a community center in a nearby city where we had regular training. The delicious meal was prepared by staff members. My favorite part of the meal was the fried chicken. Before leaving, I also received goodbye cards and letters with heartwarming notes and drawings from several of my child clients.

On my last day at the clinic in Burlingame, my brother and future sister-in-law picked me up and we attended a special event at their church in San Jose that evening. I had called my brother to confirm what time he would be at the clinic to pick me up. I didn't know it at the time, but my brother was in the middle of making wedding vows when his cell phone rang. He later told our family that he and my sister-in-law had gotten married and that I had called him in the middle of their court wedding ceremony. We all found it surprising that my brother had gotten married, and as well as comical that I had called him in the middle of his wedding vows.

Wrapping up my Practicum Training

My final practicum experience was at an agency for children and their families in Sacramento. I worked with a clinical supervisor who had her psychology license in two states. She was a great help to me, providing me with encouragement, a positive role model, and skills for my work in the future. This was a very interesting time for me. I learned of a lot of issues that occur with families and their children. I gained experience working with children and families in their home environment, as well as in the community and at the agency. I consulted with teachers, parents, parole officers, group home counselors, and community resources for families. Overall, my experience working with clients was positive.

In addition to success in my work, God blessed me with good friends to help make my experience more pleasant while accomplishing my goals. I made a few colleague friends, with whom I enjoyed time outside of and at work. One evening, before my last day at this agency, a few friends and I went to dinner. On another day before I left, a colleague and I went to lunch. On my last day, a few colleagues and I went to lunch together and when I brought my colleagues back to work after lunch, I said goodbye before going home. This was my final farewell. I was glad to have had the opportunity to spend time with my friends at work before moving on to reach further goals.

Though I had completed my practicum requirement at my final practicum site a few months earlier, I had continued to work there for a while, because I enjoyed the financial pay I was receiving. There came a time when I realized that I needed to focus my energies on completing my dissertation, so that I could graduate. I decided that my last day would be December 31st of that year.

Beginning my Formal Research

Working on my dissertation was very exciting for me. I knew what I wanted to research since my first quarter in graduate school. One of our assignments in research methods class was to develop a research design for a subject we were interested in. I had always been interested in issues regarding ethnic identity and juvenile delinquency. I developed a research design for class and the professor liked my idea and helped me present my research design to the class.

In my third quarter of school, I completed an assigned presentation in my theories of personality class. My presentation discussed my hypothesis that people who are comfortable with who they are ethnically and otherwise are less likely to be disrespectful towards others who are different. My professor talked with me during my presentation and later invited me to be a part of her research group. I accepted her invitation right away. I was very glad to be asked to be a part of a research group. I was thinking that I would have to search for and ask groups if I could join. I felt very honored that one of my professors approached me!

My research advisor was very instrumental in helping me get my research exposed. She encouraged me to be active in sharing my research findings with others. During my time in the research group, I presented at least two posters and at least two lectures. My first poster presentation was titled, "Ethnic Identity Achievement: Review of Empirical Findings." It was presented at the school's Pacific Research Forum 3rd Annual Poster Session May 21, 1999. My second poster presentation was in San Antonio, Texas, at the International Society for Traumatic Stress Studies 16th Annual Meeting November 16th-19th, 2000. Our research group met in San Antonio and presented several posters together on November 17, 2000. My poster was titled, "Trauma, Ethnic Identity, and Delinquency." I enjoyed being able to talk to others who were interested in my poster, answering questions, and exchanging interesting information. It was a very pleasant experience interacting with other professionals with similar interests and others who were simply interested in my topic of research. I enjoyed travelling to another state and presenting my poster to a whole new group of people.

My research advisor also encouraged me to present a lecture at a meeting of the Students for Ethnic and Cultural Awareness (SECA) on April 12, 2000. I presented the lecture "Factors to Consider When Surveying Multiethnic Groups." Later, I received a certificate of appreciation, signed by the SECA faculty director and the SECA President. My lecture was videotaped for the school library. I enjoyed sharing information I had discovered in my research for this lecture, which included excerpts of a documentary. As my dissertation research progressed, I was asked by my advisor to present my findings as a guest speaker to her Child, Adolescent, and Family Psychotherapy class on June 10, 2004. My topic was Ethnic Identity, focusing on the clinical implications for African Americans.

I would eventually also complete a presentation on updated research findings in relation to my dissertation at the Federal Correctional Institution of Dublin (FCI, Dublin) where I completed my pre-doctoral internship in June 2005. I was asked by my former internship supervisor to return to make a presentation to new students working at FCI, Dublin. It was a pleasant experience, talking to the new interns and exchanging questions and answers and interesting information.

Graduating with Honors

In addition to encouraging me to be proactive in presenting my research findings, my research advisor also nominated me for prestigious recognition awards for my graduate work. On May 24, 2001, I received the Brian Phillips Keith Assistantship from PGSP. During my graduation ceremony on June 11, 2005, I received the Murray Tondow Outstanding Dissertation Award! When my father and nephew opened the programs, they exclaimed, "Liz's name is on the front page!" They began going around the sanctuary collecting programs. I felt appreciated that day! I remember during my graduate work in school, my mother would tell me that I was going to graduate with honors and I would reply, "With honors?" At certain points, I thought I would barely graduate at all. My mother told me that she saw a vision of me and white lilies, which we took as a good sign. At my graduation ceremony, sure enough, there were white

Me standing by white lilies in the court yard at my graduation venue, June 2005

lilies growing in the court yard of the church where the ceremony was held. I stood right next to them, while my mother took photos of me in my graduation cap and gown.

That was a beautiful day. My parents and my sister, who had been visiting with me from Sacramento, came with me to the ceremony. My brother and his children, my nieces and nephew, came

*Me by pond in court yard at graduation venue
before the ceremony, June 2005*

Mom and Dad celebrating my graduation ceremony with me June 2005

*My sister, Alice, my brother, Johnny, and me
at my graduation celebration, June 2005*

*My niece, Demorise, my brother, Johnny, my sister, Alice, my
niece, Traevion, my nephew, Maurice, and my niece, Sonya
celebrating my graduation with me June 2005*

Me, Dad, Mom, and my niece, Demorise at my graduation celebration, June 2005

My niece, Demorise, my brother, Johnny, my nephew, Maurice, me, my niece, Sonya, and my niece Traevion at my graduation celebration, June 2005

from San Jose. Also in attendance was one of my best friends from graduate school.

Before graduating, I had an adventure completing my dissertation. I was very curious about specific issues and I was eager to find answers. I was very motivated and enthusiastic about gathering data from real people who provided their perspectives by answering surveys that I had chosen. I was very fortunate to be able to gain access to elementary, junior high, and high school students. I enjoyed setting up appointments with principals, teachers, and school administrators. Everyone was so gracious and willing to help me in my research. The students were very pleasant to work with and I was appreciative of everyone who volunteered to participate in my research project. Schools throughout the Bay Area participated. I enjoyed travelling to the schools and speaking with the students and teachers. I was thankful for help from peers in my research group, who were also surveying students.

As I mentioned earlier, graduate school was an adventure for me. Once my class schedule became fuller and I began to work at practicum and internship sites, it was necessary for me to move to the Bay Area. I moved approximately three times during my years in graduate school. Initially, my school found a dorm placement for me at Menlo Community College in Atherton, California. The college rented dorms to Stanford students as well. When I moved from Sacramento to the Menlo College dorm, I was able to pursue a full schedule of classes. Eventually, my classes were finished and my practicum site was in Burlingame. I moved to San Jose, where my parents helped me find a small studio apartment in a secured building for people on fixed income. (I was living on student loans at the time.)

When I finished my Burlingame practicum, I moved back home to live with my parents and completed the rest of my practicum work in Sacramento.

While I was living with my parents before I began my pre-doctoral training, I began preparing for my Clinical Oral Exam at school. The oral exam consisted of a panel of two staff members who would present a clinical scenario and ask questions regarding how treatment might proceed in that case. Because I had not known quite how to study for the oral exam, which might cover any area of psychology and require any variety of answers regarding several possible specialties in psychology, I once again had some difficulty passing. I remember the first oral exam I took was given by staff with specialties in neuropsychology, an area I was familiar with and in which I successfully and reasonably easily passed my courses. It was not an area of psychology that I tended to focus on, so I was not prepared for my first oral exam and did not pass. Later,

I took my oral exam for a second time; I think I should have learned a lesson from the first time and made more of an effort to study neuropsychology information, because I repeated the results of my previous oral exam. After failing my oral exam for the second time, I literally felt an ache all over my body and in my heart. One day, while visiting a shopping mall with my parents to shop and eat dinner, I purchased a consolation gift for myself. It was a little puppy with soft brown fur and floppy ears. (It was a stuffed toy. It wasn't real.) I carried my puppy around with me most everywhere I went, holding it lightly against my chest and heart where it hurt a lot.

Once I began to feel better, I organized my studies to include a larger variety of resources, including Diagnostic and Statistical Manual 4th edition (DSM-IV) study guides with scenario index cards regarding a variety of Axis I and Axis II diagnoses and clinical study guides that provided real life cases. I would read the scenarios and write out my treatment plan before reading how the cases were actually handled. I became more familiar with developing my own treatment plans and diagnoses and felt comfortable with my clinical skills.

I took my Clinical Oral Exam for the third time. This time, the testing panel consisted of staff I was more familiar with. I had been praying that God be with me to help me pass my oral exam and I could literally feel his presence with me that day. During my exam, it was as if God was speaking words through me. Everything just flowed out of my mouth and I spoke with confidence and ease. I was tremendously happy to find out that I had finally passed my oral exam. It was another huge hurdle that God helped me get over. I felt such a sense of healing and relief.

I began my pre-doctoral internship at the Federal Correctional Institution of Dublin. In order to work there, I moved to an apartment that my parents helped me find in San Ramon, California. Living in San Ramon was a fun experience. I attended a local church that was recommended by the couple I was renting from. I enjoyed attending that church and eventually joined. I became a part of the youth ministry, assisting in the children's church during evening services and every other Sunday morning. Fortunately, there were two regular services each Sunday, so on the days that I worked in the children's church, I could attend regular services afterward. I also joined the singles ministry and organized an outing to San Francisco to see the Giants play. That was unique and fun experience for me.

Working at FCI, Dublin was a nice experience. I enjoyed working with my clients and I gained experience providing crisis intervention, intake assessment and treatment planning, anger management groups, stress reduction groups, trauma treatment groups, and individual therapy. I remember having a tiny office on the second floor of a cell unit. Sometimes I would research files for psychological evaluations in a large conference room on the unit. I never felt afraid or insecure. I always felt God's presence with me. Most of my clients attended their sessions regularly and productively and seemed to appreciate my work with them. I'm glad that I had the opportunity to gain experience working at FCI, Dublin. I became acquainted with the warden, who was very nice to the psychology students. When our internship was finished, she presented each of us with a copper tinted glass mug trimmed in gold, and a silver pen with gold trim. The director of the internship program presented us with a T-shirt with the facility logo sewn onto it and a certificate of completion dated June 24, 2005. My primary supervisor was very encouraging. He used to suggest that I apply to be hired with federal corrections. I always declined. One of the main reasons was that I didn't want to combine my psychology career with becoming a police officer, learn to use weapons, or search clients, but I always appreciated being asked. It made me feel like my work was valued and I was seen as competent. My secondary supervisor helped supervision go by nicely because we usually met at Starbuck's. I didn't mind that at all. She provided encouraging feedback and advice for the improvement of my clinical skills. There were also several other friendly staff members who provided helpful supervision and with whom I enjoyed eating lunch in the staff lounge.

My overall experience in graduate school was pleasant. When it was time to apply to post-doctoral internships, I received letters of recommendation from my research advisor at PGSP, one of my professors at PGSP who also served on my dissertation committee, my primary supervisor at FCI, Dublin, my primary supervisor at the family clinic in Burlingame, and my clinical supervisor at the practicum site in Sacramento.

As a result of being a part of my research group, I was published three times. My dissertation, "Relationships between ethnic Identity, trauma Symptoms, and juvenile Delinquency," was published December 13, 2005. In 2007, I contributed to an article, "The Role of Ethnic Identity in the Relationship of Race-Related Stress to PTSD Symptoms among Young Adults," in the Journal of Trauma and Dissociation volume 9, pages 91–105. In 2008, my article, "Relationships of Ethnicity, Ethnic Identity, and Trauma Symptoms to Delinquency," was published in the Journal of Loss and Trauma volume 13, pages 395–405.

ALL THIS FOR ME?

My Life Immediately Following Graduate School

I had not realized it was coming, until it came over me before I knew it. From the period of June 11, 2005 through February 13, 2006, I was about to receive a great deal of publicity and positive attention for my accomplishments in graduate school. I had been so used to quietly working hard in order to reach my goals that I was almost overwhelmed (in a good way) when suddenly I was getting love and encouragement from people I never knew! It was a wonderful feeling to be so admired just for accomplishing one of my life long goals. I knew I would be happy, but I didn't know so many others would be happy for me too. (Love is in the world!) It was a wonderful, exciting, and surreal time in my life.

It all began one day when I was in the school library at PGSP working at a computer. My research advisor came over to me and informed me that I would be receiving an award for my dissertation and that my award would include $1000. I was so shocked. I think I hardly knew how to breathe for a few seconds. I think I almost cried. It was such pleasant and unexpected news. Finding out about my upcoming award made the rest of my day. I felt a sense of relief and joy that my work was actually recognized and appreciated to such a degree!

A few days later, I was informed by a school administrator that I would be receiving a call from a newspaper columnist to schedule an interview regarding my accomplishments at PGSP and my award for an outstanding dissertation. I was very happy to talk to the news reporter, sharing with her everything I could think of that would be helpful in her news column about my story. I enjoyed my interview and we scheduled a time that a news photographer would meet me to take a photograph of me for my story. I was very excited and I picked out something to wear that I thought would look professional and photograph well. I chose one of my favorite outfits at the time. It was a blue dress suit with a sleeveless dress that was worn under a long overcoat. It kind of reminded me of a physician's coat. When the news photographer called, we agreed to meet at my home to take the photo. He arrived on a beautiful sunny day and I thought about possibly taking the photo outside by the trees or flowers. I even considered taking the photo by the pool. After exploring our options, the photographer and I agreed to take my photograph inside for a more professional look. I sat at my dining room table with my dissertation award plaque displayed in front of me on top of several academic texts, including a journal of psychotropic medications, the DSM-IV, and a clinical case book. The photographer and I thought this pose might help convey the spirit behind my story. I was pleased with the newspaper column written by the columnist who interviewed me and with my photograph in vivid color on the front page! My story was featured in several newspapers around the Bay Area, including the Sunday, July 10, 2005 edition of the Oakland Tribune, the Monday, July 11, 2005 edition of the San Ramon Valley Herald, and later an additional extension of my story in the Sunday, January 29, 2006 edition of the San Ramon Valley Herald The Valley.

My story in the newspaper captured much positive attention. I received cards and letters from private citizens in the Bay Area through the care of my school and I received phone calls from Bay Area Universities of California regarding possible post-doctoral fellowships, including UC San Francisco. I even had a few informal conversations with an African American professor at UC Berkeley. I also received inquiries regarding possible speaking engagements at churches. I remember trying to balance keeping track of my new well-wishing and encouraging acquaintances with my focus on obtaining post-doctoral training.

A Slight Mistake

After accepting a post-doctoral position at a small clinic in Berkeley, I began attending orientation and preliminary training there. One day on my way back home to San Ramon, I was riding the Bay Area Rapid Transit (BART) train when my cell phone rang. (Looking back, I probably should not have tried to answer my cell phone while riding the train. There were many distractions, such as noise, lack of privacy, and less ability to think clearly, especially coming home from a busy day.) I answered my cell phone, and it was a person from Kaiser Medical center in Fremont, offering me a chance to interview for a post-doctoral position. I wasn't thinking very clearly and I wasn't sure that I would get the position. The train was a bit loud, and I think I said, "Huh?" a few times. I informed the person that I had obtained a post-doctoral position and was currently working in that capacity already, but that I could accept a part-time position as an employee at the medical center. I was informed that there were no part-time positions available. I declined the interview at that time. A few days later, after I thought about it, I could not believe what I had done. Eventually, I decided to discontinue my post-doctoral training at the smaller clinic and pursue another chance at a post-doctoral position at Kaiser Medical center in Fremont. I was able to contact the person who made the initial offer to me, but I was informed that the position was no longer available.

Getting my Mind off of Myself

It was around this time that Hurricane Katrina happened in New Orleans, Louisiana. The East Bay Community Law Center, located near the small clinic where I was receiving post-doctoral training, was accepting charity donations for the people of New Orleans. I wanted to help somehow and I was glad to discover a way I could help as best I could. I donated a few coats that I thought would be nice gifts, dropping them off at the community law center. I was able to talk to a few people at the center who shared that the donations were going to be driven by truck to locations in New Orleans where people needed them. I was glad to be a part of such a demonstration of love to others. I later received two thank you cards for my donations.

More Blessings

Before I discontinued my post-doctoral position at the smaller clinic in Berkeley, I was able to make a few friends there. One of my closer friends and I would sometimes meet for lunch or dinner in the downtown Berkeley area. One evening while I was at home, I received a phone call. It was my friend who sounded somewhat perplexed. When I asked her what was going on, she said, "I was looking through my psychology magazine subscription, and I see your freaking picture on the front page!" I started laughing hysterically at my friend's reaction to seeing me in a magazine published by the American Psychological Association (APA). I explained to her that my school had awarded me for an outstanding dissertation and my story had been published in the newspaper and more recently in editions of APA published magazines. The publication I purchased for myself was the November 2005, volume 36, No. 10 American Psychological Association MONITOR ON PSYCHOLOGY.

My story in the APA magazine was another unexpected blessing that overtook me before I knew it. One day after walking to my car once I got off the BART train, I was sitting in my car in the parking lot. I was getting ready to start my car and head home when my cell phone rang. It was a person from the APA magazine. The person asked me, "When will we be receiving a photo from you?" I asked, "What kind of photo would you like and what is the photo for?" The person informed me that my photo was needed for a feature of PGSP in the APA magazine publication. I replied, "Okay, I'll get a photo for you. Where can I send it?" I chose a recent photograph that was professionally done previously when my mother and I were walking through a mall and were randomly chosen to receive a free photo session at a photography studio. We took full advantage of the opportunity to a have free photo session. My mother gave her coupon to my sister and my sister and I had our photos taken soon afterward. (Of course, once I saw all of the photographs, I couldn't just take the free one, I had to purchase the entire photo shoot.)

After choosing a photograph that I thought would be the most appropriate for my feature story in the APA magazine, I was happy to send it in. I couldn't wait until my story was published in the magazine so I could purchase a copy for myself. Once I purchased my copy of the magazine, I felt so honored to be featured on the second page inside the magazine cover. I almost felt like an actual prominent member of the clinical elite in psychology society.

The Waiting Begins

After discontinuing my post-doctoral position at the clinic in Berkeley, I continued to pursue post-doctoral training at sites more similar to the one I had declined at the Kaiser Medical Center, Fremont. There was a period when I did not receive any responses. Furthermore, my student loan was going to end soon and I needed financial income. I eventually applied for and received an additional private loan. I was looking for a post-doctoral position that would allow me to work part time if the position did not pay so that I could have a part-time job. I could not find a full-time paying post-doctoral position, nor could I find a part-time non-paying position that would allow me time to work at a paying job.

Fortunately, I was able to find a temporary job at a data entry service. The job allowed me to earn enough income for gas and food. My parents were paying for most of my financial obligations during this time in my life which I called the "wilderness." I told my parents that I believed I was wandering in the wilderness due to some poor decisions I recently made. I was angry at myself for having lost the opportunity to work at Kaiser Medical Center, Fremont. It took me quite a while to get over it. The manager who hired me at the data entry job was very nice. He was a Christian, like me, and we sometimes discussed our faith in God and mutual interests in Christian music. He did not realize everything I was going through. I guess during the months I worked there, I had lost a significant amount of weight without noticing it myself. One day the manager asked to talk with me privately. When I went to speak with him, he informed me that he and my supervisor were very concerned about my health. He stated, "You have lost a lot of weight since you started here and you did not have the weight to lose." After I heard his concern, I was relieved and I started laughing. I tried to explain to him that I was okay, and that I was probably not eating as much as I used to, because I was so focused on trying to find a post-doctoral placement. I don't think he believed me, or could really hear what I was trying to explain to him. I couldn't stop laughing, but he kept looking at me very seriously, stating, "Let me tell you what I tell my son all the time. If there is anything you need to have, it is balance." I was agreeing with him and I kept reassuring him that I was fine and that I would be okay. When the conversation ended, I'm pretty sure he thought I was a little mentally imbalanced. I think the manager and my supervisor may have been concerned that I might have had some sort of an eating disorder or drug problem. Starting the next morning and for several days following when I arrived at work, a small snack, consisting of cheese crackers and a banana, was on my desk. I enjoyed my personal snack when I came in each morning. When the snacks stopped, I asked my supervisor what had happened to my morning snacks. The snacks resumed for a few more days before finally ending. The manager eventually moved back home to another state. I remained at the job a few weeks longer, before moving back home with my parents in Sacramento.

I tried so hard to remain in the Bay Area and find a post-doctoral position, but it just wasn't happening. I even considered renting a room from a home owner I located online. I went to view the home in Fremont and was seriously contemplating living in a bedroom at a stranger's home. I told the home owner that I would bring my parents and get their opinions. My parents came to San Ramon to visit me and view the home I was thinking of moving into in Fremont. They were saying, "No way" as soon as we parked in front of the home. We almost didn't go in. After viewing the home, my parents were very confident that their answer was "No." My parents helped me search for other living options in the tri-valley area. We seriously considered a trailer home for me, which we thought would be less expensive. When my mother saw that I was so resolute on not moving back home to Sacramento, she warned me that she saw an eviction notice on my door in a dream. I asked my mother, "Would an eviction notice be on my financial record?" She replied, "Yes, It would." While I was thinking, my mother stated, "You don't have to move all of your furniture and bed back home. You can come home until you find a post-doctoral position." This idea was like a light bulb for me, because one of the things I dreaded was having to move all of my things back and forth. The thought of just having myself to move around was much easier for me. I replied, "Yeah, That's right! I can leave my furniture and things here in storage, until I'm ready for them again!" We agreed that I would move back home again until I found suitable post-doctoral training. Soon after our decision, I received two prospective offers, one at Napa State Hospital and one at Kaiser Medical Center in Redwood City! I pursued both opportunities. In the meantime, I moved back home with my parents.

Before I moved away, I was able to say goodbye to the couple I rented my apartment from during my time in San Ramon. I updated them on how things were going and about my two prospective opportunities in Napa and Red Wood City. They were happy for me and stated that the Napa area was very beautiful and I would enjoy living there. I agreed and thought it would be very nice to live in such an area. Several other people had similar reactions when I told them of my prospective opportunities.

Another Sign of God's Favor with Me

While I still lived in San Ramon, I received continued encouraging publicity. I was contacted by the Founder and President of the African American Ethnic Sports Hall of Fame. I was chosen to be a recipient of the Personal Education Award.

I couldn't believe it. I was receiving more community support. I was featured in the newspaper again in the Sunday, January 29, 2006 edition of the San Ramon Herald The Valley on the front page! This time the story included my acceptance of the African American Ethnic Sports Hall of Fame Personal Education Award. It felt great!

Of course, I accepted my award in person. The ceremony was held on February 10, 2006 at the Hyatt San Jose in San Jose, California, for the Annual Bay Area Induction. It was a beautiful evening. My parents attended the ceremony with me. Prior to the formal ceremony and dinner, there was an informal reception in another dining area. My parents and I were enjoying light appetizers when, guess who sat at our table with us. It was a former Raiders football player. He was also receiving an award that evening. He was very pleasant and down to earth. My parents and I enjoyed sitting and talking with him before the formal ceremony began. We took pictures with him and he signed my program for the evening. I still have all of my souvenirs from that evening, even my name tag that was the center piece that reserved our table in the main event dining room and my reception speech notes. A few days after the event, I received a letter from the Founder and President of the African American Ethnic Sports Hall of Fame thanking me for attending the event. I kept that letter also.

While becoming acquainted at the African American Ethnic Sports Hall of Fame event, my parents and I found out that our new acquaintance was a former Raiders teammate of the pastor of the church I had joined in Dublin, California, The Well. I enjoyed attending The Well during my time living in San Ramon. The pastor always had encouraging words and was glad to see great things happen to other people. When my story was in the newspaper, the pastor acknowledged me in front of the congregation on a Sunday morning and the congregation expressed happiness for me with cheers and clapping. He also stated that I would probably become more renowned in the future. When the church was honoring graduates, I received a professional pen/pencil/calculator set as a graduation gift, after my graduation from PGSP. A few months later, the pastor prophesied that I would be financially free to build my own youth and family clinic without financial debt and be able to give money to others without having to borrow. That was a prophecy I gladly received as confirmation that all of my dreams would come true.

GOD IS HOLDING MY HAND

*Completing my Post-doctoral Training and
California License to Practice Clinical Psychology*

*J*n the Interim between the end of my pre-
doctoral internship and moving back
home with my parents in Sacramento, I
was invited for an interview at Napa State Hospital and was
very excited to go. I made the trip to my interview by bus,
which included connections with the local bus line in the
Napa area, called the Grapeline. I remember riding through
fields of vineyards and taking the view in from my window
on the small bus. I arrived quite early for my appointment,
so once I became acquainted with the campus enough to

confirm the appropriate location for the interview, I walked to McDonald's and had breakfast. When I arrived for my interview after breakfast, I met the doctor who arranged the interview with me. He guided me into a room, where I was taken by surprise to find a panel of staff members sitting around a table where there was also a seat for me. This was my first time interviewing for a state job, so I was not aware it would be a clinical exam! In my brain, the interview was going to be a pleasant conversation for the interviewers to find out more about my skills and interests and for me to ask questions about the interviewers' expectations and desires for a new employee. I was quickly made aware that my clinical skills were about to be revealed in a moment of truth! If I knew that I would be taking an exam, I would have prepared a bit differently. Nevertheless, I tried to hide my surprise and I was able to keep my composure. The staff on the panel were very friendly, polite, and patient. They gave me several clinical case scenarios and asked me how I would proceed with diagnosis and treatment in each case. The exam was recorded and there was a tape recorder in front of me on the table which added to my very slight case of nerves. Anyway, I completed the exam as best I could and was hopeful that I presented myself as a competent clinician. I said goodbye to the staff and headed back home. It was a generally quiet and peaceful day with the sun shining and the climate just right – not too hot or too cold. I arrived home wondering how I was perceived during my interview/exam. After a few days, I received notice of my exam results in the mail. I was relieved to see that I had a marginally decent grade. I passed my exam with a 70%. I was content with my results, considering I had not been prepared for my interview the way I would have liked. I was notified that I was now eligible for future exams, as long as I remained available and was interested in available positions. This was good news for me to hear as well. I had not heard further from Napa State Hospital and gathered that I probably was not being considered for hire there.

I began preparing to move back home with my parents in Sacramento. I located a storage facility in San Ramon where I moved car loads of my belongings whenever I had free time. I usually made several trips back and forth, taking items to storage. When I told a close friend at church I was moving, she offered to help. One sunny Saturday morning, after we attended a women's meeting at church, my friend brought her pick-up truck and helped me move items to storage. For my large furniture, such as my couches, I hired professional movers, who wrapped my furniture in protective plastic before moving it. Soon after I was ready, my parents came to San Ramon by train for me. We loaded the final items into my car, I said goodbye to a neighbor, and my parents and I headed for Sacramento, my father driving.

Hope for another Chance

I was living at home a few weeks after submitting an application to Kaiser Medical center in Redwood City and received a request for further information. I was beginning to wonder if I still had a chance of becoming a post-doctoral fellow there. I was waiting hopefully and optimistically. One day I contacted by phone the Director of the Department of Psychiatry, who had initially contacted me. He informed me that applicants were still being considered. He instructed me to call him every week at a specific time as long as I was interested in the post-doctoral internship. I agreed. I wasn't quite sure how to take my instructions and I consulted with my parents. My father and I were thinking that maybe the director was not very interested in me after all, or he would have just accepted me into the internship program. We thought it might not be a good idea to keep calling him. My mother pointed out that I should not be too proud to keep calling. She pointed out, "Usually, when people are not interested, they'll say, 'Don't call us. We'll call you.'" My mother advised me that I should take advantage of the chance and keep calling the director every week. He probably wanted to see how much I wanted the position. My father and I agreed with my mother and we realized, "That's true. They do usually say, 'Don't call us. We'll call you,' but he said 'Keep calling!' He didn't have to say that!" I called the director of the psychiatry department at Kaiser Medical Center in Redwood City every week at the same time, without fail, continuing to be hopeful that I would be accepted as a post-doctoral fellow. When he did not answer, I would leave a voicemail, "Hello, Doctor, This is Elizabeth Bruce, calling to let you know that I am still interested in a post-doctoral internship."

During my months at home, between my pre-doctoral and post-doctoral internships, Joel Osteen came to the Arco arena in Sacramento. When I found out, I knew I wanted to attend in person. The conference was free and I only had to pay $10 for parking at the arena. I learned of the upcoming Joel Osteen event one Sunday at the church I frequently attend with my parents in Sacramento, Capital Christian Center. Free tickets were being provided to the Joel Osteen event and I made sure I was in line to get a ticket.

I got another Chance!

On the night of the Joel Osteen event, I waited in line to enter the arena and chatted a little with friendly people around me. Once I found my seat, I relaxed and waited for the service to start. The lights were very low, so I felt comfortable and I wasn't self-conscious, because the spot light was on the stage. I arrived at the event significantly early, so I had not decided to turn my cell phone off yet. While I was in anticipation of praising the Lord, my cell phone rang. It was a doctor (who would eventually be my primary supervisor) from Kaiser Medical Center in Redwood City, calling to set up an interview appointment with me! I could not believe it. It had finally happened. I was finally being seriously considered for a post-doctoral internship at a Kaiser medical center! It was a huge relief. I felt like I had gotten a second chance after I missed my first chance. The waiting was over. After scheduling an interview appointment over the phone, I called my parents before the Joel Osteen service began. My parents were happy for me and congratulated me. Eventually more people began to gather in the arena and a family sat next to me. The family was very friendly and the mother and father introduced themselves and their children. The mother and I talked about the goodness of God and things we looked forward to enjoying during the service. It was a very nice atmosphere of peace and worship. When the service started and the praise and worship team came out on stage, I could feel the presence of the Lord, as the entire arena lifted Him up in worship. After the phone call from the doctor, the evening was enhanced for me and I knew I had the favor of the Lord to continue my progress toward fulfilling his purpose for me.

I began my work as a psychological assistant at Kaiser Medical Center, Redwood City in September of 2006 and completed my internship in October 2007. During my time there, I enjoyed training in a wide variety of areas within the field of psychology. It was exciting to be able to participate in treatment for clients in a variety of settings and using a variety of treatment techniques and strategies. I was able to make hospital rounds with a neuropsychologist, who was one of my supervisors. I observed him on rounds to assess patients being treated for brain injuries. I was allowed to sit in on rounds with physicians, as they discussed client cases.

I was able to assist one of my supervisors in the clinic for Attention Deficit Hyperactivity Disorder (ADHD), where I learned skills in assessing clients for ADHD. My supervisor allowed me to facilitate a treatment group for ADHD patients, provide intake assessments for patients who were concerned they might have ADHD or who were referred to the ADHD clinic, and write psychological evaluations for the treatment of patients.

I also received supervised experience working with the director of the psychiatry department. I participated in the psychiatry department intake clinic with the director, assessing, diagnosing, and developing treatment plans for new patients. I also co-facilitated anxiety treatment groups with the director.

My primary supervisor gave me the opportunity to work with couples in therapy and work individually with clients in the anxiety clinic. I was very pleasantly surprised when I received a letter of commendation from one of my patients, who wrote the letter to my supervisor. When she gave me the letter, I had not realized it was coming. It was a very nice feeling to know that one of my patients felt so positively toward me. I was also given the opportunity to assist in crisis interventions for patients who needed emergency admittance to the psychiatric hospital. I gained experience in the procedure of assessing patients, interacting with family, and interacting with the police in crisis situations.

I was able to work with supervisors from a variety of cultural backgrounds. My secondary supervisor helped me learn cultural factors of working with Latino clients and I was able to have many interesting clinical discussions with him on a variety of topics. I also had an African American supervisor who I could relate to on many levels. She gave me encouraging advice and a text book, which I later used for developing treatment plans for patients after my work at Kaiser Medical Center, Redwood City was complete.

While working at Kaiser Medical Center, Redwood City, I gained experience working in a Dialectical Behavior Treatment (DBT) group with two supervisors who I observed co-facilitate the group. One co-facilitator gave me several relaxation tapes that I gave to my mother who really enjoyed using them with our family. My mother also gave one of the tapes to a friend. The other co-facilitator was also friendly, and we frequently enjoyed conversations together during leisure breaks.

In addition to psychologists, I was able to develop friendly professional acquaintances with psychiatrists, who were very helpful to me in consultations regarding patient treatment. I really enjoyed being able to consult with experts in other specialties. I enjoyed my experience at Kaiser Medical Center, Redwood City.

Personal Living

During my internship at Kaiser Medical Center, Redwood City, I also enjoyed living in San Mateo. I attended a local church and met the pastor, who I eventually introduced to a friend from graduate school who was visiting me. At the local church, I became friends with a very nice couple who used to sit in the same section as me during services on Sundays. My parents also attended church with me when they visited me over weekends. When I was alone, I frequently visited the local library to read about and research topics I found interesting. One weekend, I attended an event called the Soul Stroll. It was a very nice way for me to get out and get exercise, doing something different. I met up with a large group of people who were also participating at Coyote Point Park on Saturday, May 19, 2007, 10:00AM – 1:00PM. The event was sponsored by the African American Community Health Advisory with Mills-Peninsula Health Services. After a continental breakfast and a brief warm-up exercise on the grass with inspirational music, we began our hike through the hills and forest. We were able to choose how far we wanted to hike. We could turn around at one of several points depending on how far we wanted our entire hike to be. I think I hiked a total of 26 miles. It was a fun adventure for me. I was taking pictures throughout my hike. I remember hearing a few people whispering comments like, "She's acting like a tourist." I didn't care about these comments. I was taking everything in, the sights of nature, the weather, the walk, and the friendly people I met during my walk. I enjoyed it all. That day was very nice. The sun was shining beautifully. It wasn't too hot and a breeze was blowing, but it wasn't too cold. When we made it back to the meeting place at Coyote Point Park, we each got honorary medals around our necks and a tote bag of small gifts and informational booklets. We also had a nice lunch. I was able to make positive memories of San Mateo before moving back home once again to live with my parents in Sacramento.

Back to the Task of Searching for Post-doctoral Training

Prior to completing my year at Kaiser Medical Center, Redwood City, I had already begun the search for my next field of training to complete my final 500 hours of post-doctoral internship. I was looking for a site where I could be hired as an employee, earning a salary while completing my post-doctoral requirement. My father helped me look for employment. One day he was on his computer and he announced, "The state is hiring and they have a lot of positions available for psychologists. You could probably find a job easily with the state and they are advertising that in many areas homes are very inexpensive." My immediate response was, "Yes, I could buy my own house!" After thinking about it for a while, my mother and I told my father that I probably would not want to live "way out in the desert" by myself in a strange place. A few days later, when I was visiting my parents in my room at home, my mother came in. She said, "You know Liz, I was just thinking, 'That girl is going to have bills to pay, and I'm not going to be able to pay them for her.' Maybe you should look into the state jobs after all." I started laughing immediately and replied, "That's true! I'm going to have a lot of bills to pay, and I would like to be able to have a new home. I'm going to check into the jobs Dad told me about." I asked my father how I could begin applying for state jobs and he gave me the website to go online. I applied for all of the state jobs I could find with vacancies for psychologists. I received plenty of positive responses and chances to interview. I was very hopeful and excited. I pursued the first opportunity for an interview. It was from a state facility in Porterville, California. None of us had ever heard of Porterville before. I asked my father to help me find it on a large map posted on a wall in our home office. My father and I were surprised to find that Porterville was actually located on the map. My mother was a member of Curves at the time. I visited a Curves exercise center with her one day and was thinking of joining; but we didn't know if there would be a Curves where I was moving. My mother and I talked with a Curves representative at the center where we had exercised that day. The representative located several Curves locations in Porterville! We were surprised again. I guess we were really imagining that I would be out in the middle of nowhere.

After my online application for a psychologist position at the state facility was completed on September 17, 2007, I was contacted by personnel on September 20, 2007. I was asked to send in my academic transcripts. On September 22, 2007, I requested an academic transcript from graduate school. On

October 2, 2007, a letter was written to me with an appointment time for an oral interview/examination on Thursday, October 11, 2007, at 10AM with Panel #1. This time I was prepared for an oral exam and was ready to go! I informed my parents of the good news and prepared for my trip by Greyhound to Porterville, California.

On the day of my trip, I rode Greyhound to Goshen, California, where there was a 3-hour layover at a very small Greyhound station. Fortunately, I happened to meet another very nice lady, who happened to be on her way to the same place I was going to have my interview. She was a Christian and we had a few things in common. We were able to pass the time in pleasant conversation. When the Greyhound bus arrived, it took us to a bus depot in Porterville, where we parted ways. She went to the state facility and I went to the motel I where I would be spending the night before my interview the next morning.

After a good night's sleep, I woke up to get ready for my interview in a few hours. I checked out of the motel and walked to the nearby bus stop where a local bus would pick me up and drop me off at the front entrance of the facility. I walked into the administration building and searched for the designated meeting place. I located the appropriate meeting place and checked in at a reception office located behind a half door, with the bottom portion closed and the top portion open. I waited in the hallway on a bench near the interview room. When it was time for my interview, one of the staff on the interview panel came to greet me and guide me to the interview room. The panel consisted of approximately five staff members from various offices within the administration of the facility. Because I had interviewed for state employment before, I was more prepared for a panel, exam questions, and being tape recorded. I felt I had a good rapport with the panel members and I was glad to be getting this chance to demonstrate that I would be an asset as an employee.

After the interview/exam was over, I and a few other examinees were invited to take a tour of the facility. This gave me hope that I was being considered seriously for employment. While we waited for our tour guide, one of the members of the panel came to sit with us in the waiting area of the administration building. Once the tour began, we were taken around the facility campus and were able to meet staff and residents. It was like its own little city. After my visit to my prospective employment site, I was very enthusiastic and optimistic. While standing at a bus stop to begin my trip home, I took a picture with my cell phone of the desert land across the street from the bus stop and happily sent it to my parents, saying, "Here is where I am in Porterville, See?" This is across the street from the bus stop I'm waiting at." Later when I talked to my parents about my trip, we were all laughing because I sent them a picture of dirt and rocks, and said, "See? This is Porterville."

I received my examination results in a letter dated October 15, 2007, three days after my interview. I achieved a passing score of 82% and I was very happy! Now all I had to do was wait to hear further information regarding my eligibility for hire. I knew others had also taken the exam and I didn't know how my scores compared with theirs. I received an employment inquiry letter, dated October 18, 2007, informing me that I was successful in my examination and instructing me to complete an attached application and submit it before October 29, 2007 if I was still interested in the psychologist position. I completed my application on October 20, 2007. I was really excited and very hopeful I was going to be hired very soon. Eventually, I was contacted to set an appointment date for an interview/examination with a second panel, which would consist of staff working in the department I was being considered for. It seemed like forever between my first interview and my second, but looking back at the time line, it could not have been more than a few weeks. I remember telling my mother that it took me a year to find a job. She pointed out, "It didn't take that long at all. Maybe a few weeks, but not a year!"

I made another happy trip to Porterville for my second interview/exam. I was relieved to discover that I did not have any competition that day, because I was the only one who arrived for an interview. Now I was very hopeful I would get the job! The second panel who interviewed me consisted of staff members I would be working with if I were to be hired. I felt confident in my responses and had a good feeling about the interview. I was asked to wait in the front lobby as the panel discussed my exam results. Eventually, one of the panel members, a nursing coordinator, came out and said to me, "I told her to hire you." I laughed and said, "Okay." Then the program director came out and said, "He didn't tell me anything." I laughed and said, "Okay." It was confirmed that I was accepted for employment! I finally had a permanent job! I would begin work on January 2, 2008.

Settling in at a New Job in a New City
The program director helped me make arrangements to rent an apartment on campus until I was able to find my own residence in the community. I was able to pick up my apartment key from the receptionist desk on December 29, 2007, the Saturday before New Year's Eve. (On New Year's Eve, I went to a local theatre to see a movie featuring Will Smith, called, *I Am Legend*. I enjoyed the movie and it helped the time alone go by easily for

me.) My parents helped me move Saturday, before going home the next day.

My father drove us from Sacramento to Porterville in my car with essential items packed that I would need. Fortunately, the apartment was furnished with beds, dressers, a couch, a dining table, a stove, and a refrigerator. I was able to keep my personal furniture in storage until I found my own place. As my parents were helping me settle into my apartment, we all noticed how cold it was and that the heater was not working. We asked for help at the receptionist desk to see how I could get the heater repaired in my apartment. The receptionist was very friendly and helped us make arrangements to for maintenance staff to repair the heater in my apartment. She and I remained friendly acquaintances throughout my years at the facility. The maintenance workers were also friendly each time they visited my apartment on campus to repair the heater or air conditioner.

I ended up staying in my campus apartment for a full year. The rent was very reasonable and I was able to pay rent, after pay days, at the trust office in the administration building. The apartments are not intended for long-term residence and I was initially thinking that I would have my own residence after three months. However, things kept coming up that would delay my move and I kept having to ask for extensions of time to stay. I was very excited about having a nice job and living on my own in a new city. I began shopping for a new home. After finding a home I was interested in, I began negotiations with the builder to have a home built within five months. I promised the program director that I just needed five more months, before I would be living in the new home I was having built. I also told friends at work about my prospective new home. However, negotiations with the builder were a struggle and even after the home was built, obstacles arose that were out of my control. I had to get out of that situation right away! I was able to get most of my money back and end negotiations with that builder before it was too late.

Nevertheless, I had to ask for yet another extension to stay on campus while I found a place of my own. I requested a three month extension. One day in February 2009, I was resting on my bed in the apartment on campus when a lady who worked in house-keeping knocked on my door. When I opened the door, she informed me that she was told that the apartment was now empty, and that she had been assigned to clean it. I informed her that I had received permission to remain in the apartment for another month. The lady politely apologized and left. From that moment on, I became determined to find a place of my own as soon as possible! That day I began looking for apartments in the community. I was able to schedule several appointments and look at several apartments. Eventually, I was able to contact an apartment manager who said she had two vacant apartments available. I visited the apartment building, toured the apartments with the manager, chose the apartment I wanted to rent, and signed a rental contract in the same day. After getting the key to my new apartment, I began moving my things from my campus apartment. By the time I moved from campus, I had accumulated a few more heavy items, so I recruited the help of a friend from work to move larger items, such as my television, boxes full of dishes, and other items.

During the year I lived on campus, I had become more acquainted with the city of Porterville. I had found a local storage facility that was significantly less expensive than my storage facility in San Ramon; I visited the city library frequently; I was shopping at a local grocery store regularly; I found my banking facility locally; and I attended a local church regularly. The pastors of the church I attended were a very friendly couple, who treated me like family. They even drove me around town to look at prospective homes to purchase. I had dinner at their home several times and felt like I had found true friends. We stayed in contact for a short period after I moved to another location and no longer attended services there.

Now that I had found an apartment off campus, I needed to have my personal furniture out of storage. My furniture and items had been in a storage facility in San Ramon before it was moved to a local storage facility with the help of my family. I rented a U-Haul truck and my father, brother, and nephew packed my storage items into the U-Haul truck and drove from the San Ramon storage facility to the local storage facility in Porterville. My father drove in my parents' car with my mother and my brother drove the truck with my nephew. We all met at the storage facility in Porterville to unpack the truck and move my items into my storage rental area. My brother had called me on the cell phone to let me know he would be hungry and to bring some food. I picked up meals for everyone at Long John Silver's before meeting them at the storage site. When I arrived, everyone was there, ready to transfer my things into storage, but they wanted to eat first! I opened the rental space and we all started work as we were ready. My mother and father told me a funny story of how my brother sped past them on the freeway, driving in the truck and waving as he passed. My parents said, "How did he pass us?" My family has always been a great support for me whenever I needed emotional, financial, or practical support. This was a time when I needed serious practical support!

I was able to keep my items in the local storage facility at a reasonable price for several months. Once I found an apartment and was ready to move my items out of the storage facility, the behavior of the facility administrators became shady and I was accused of being behind on my payments. As proof of timely payment, I made copies of my check duplicates and I informed them that I would consider my items as being held hostage if I had to seek legal help. Thank God, things cleared up after that and I was able to safely move my things out of the storage facility. When the movers arrived, I informed them that I was donating my two sofas so they would not have to be moved. One of the movers asked if he could have them and I said, "Sure." I called and cancelled my previous donation pick up appointment. The movers moved everything from the storage facility to my new apartment. This time around, it was necessary to hire movers, because everything was happening sort of fast, and I could not give my family enough notice to help me move; however, I did receive much needed advice and support from my father over the phone regarding the storage issue.

During my first week at work, I received all day training in new employee orientation (NEO). I started work during the winter and mornings were very foggy. I actually got lost on campus my first day of work, driving from my campus apartment to the administration building, because I could not see the buildings clearly. Once I was finally able to find the administration building and go inside, a very nice janitor helped me find out where I was supposed to be for training. It was in another building, across the street from the administration building. The janitor and I remained friendly acquaintances during my time at the state facility, saying hello whenever we passed each other in the halls of the administration offices.

During NEO, I and other new employees were provided with training regarding how to remain safe while working, appropriate interactions with clients, communication skills, background information about the facility, CPR, and first aid training. The training was very helpful in preparing me for my new environment.

I was assigned to a unit in the secure treatment area, behind a locked fence, with a sally port that we had to go through for police officers to check for contraband items, before we were allowed through. My duties on the unit included psychological evaluations, court reports, developing behavior modification plans, and consulting with interdisciplinary team members regarding the behavior and treatment plans for clients. In addition to general supervision from the program director, I received clinical supervision from the senior psychologist, who also assigned a secondary clinical supervisor who helped me in my clinical work.

More Positive Recognition

Having this job was a great opportunity for me. Not only was I able to complete my final hours of post-doctoral training, I was also hired as a permanent employee. One day, after I had been working a little longer than a year, I received a pleasant surprise in my mailbox in the program office. It was a certificate that read "Employee Parking Pass This Certificate is Awarded to Elizabeth Bruce, Ph.D. Valid March 1 thru March 31, 2009, Program IX management, PD." The Program Director named me as employee of the month! That was a great feeling. Even though it was very annoying to arrive at work many mornings to find that someone had parked in my designated spot, it was nice that I was recognized as employee of the month. That was the important matter.

Passing my Psychology License Exams

I began studying for my license exams after completing my post-doctoral training. In order to earn a license with the California Board of Psychology, I was required to pass the Examination for Professional Practice in Psychology (EPPP) and the California Psychology Supplemental Exam (CPSE). When I was hired, I was allotted three years to earn my license in order to remain classified as a psychologist at the facility. I had completed my post-doctoral hours within my first year of hire (2008) and I planned to study a year before taking my license exams (2009). I extended my study time a few months until I felt like I was ready to take my first exam, the EPPP. To assist me in obtaining my license within my three-year time frame, I was given 5 paid hours per week to study for my license exams. I was able to come home early from work on Mondays in order to study. My personal study schedule that I made was four hours each day on the weekends, my days off, and every Monday. I used a study package that I purchased from an agency that sells test preparation materials for license exams. It included text booklets from each area of psychology, practice quizzes, practice exams, timed computer exams, CD lectures in each area of psychology, and live seminars. The package was very helpful for me in managing my study focus, sorting out my study time, and prioritizing areas I needed improvement in.

I took the EPPP at the end of the year in 2009. It was during a foggy season and the testing site was in Fresno, California. My parents were concerned about me driving for an hour in the fog, so they came to spend a few days with me in Porterville and drive me to Fresno on my exam day. My exam would be a few hours, so my parents dropped me off at my testing site and spent the day in Fresno while I took my exam. As I sat in my testing cubicle, I felt rather confident and relatively relaxed. The questions seemed reasonable and I was pretty sure of my accuracy in answering them. As time went on, however, I began to doze off. I am not sure why. I think it may have been my nerves. Anyway, I found myself waking up just as test time had expired. I had approximately ten more items to answer, but it was too late to finish them. I could not believe I had dozed off and slept through the final minutes of my exam! I remained hopeful that I had passed. I prayed to God, "Lord, I know I slept at the end of my exam, but please make me pass anyway!" I told my parents what had happened and they encouraged me, letting me know that I still had a very good chance of passing.

I had an overall feeling of confidence about the way I performed on my exam and was optimistic about getting my test results. I would check my post office mailbox every day at lunch time during work. The senior psychologist would ask me how I did on my exam. I would reply, "I have not received my results yet." One day when I opened my mailbox, I found the letter I had been waiting for. It was from the department of consumer affairs. When I got into my car I opened the letter, dated 1/4/10, to find wonderful news. I had passed my EPPP! The letter informed me that I passed with a score of 577 and the passing score was 500. The Lord had answered my prayers! I passed, even though I fell asleep during my exam! I immediately called the senior psychologist at work and told him that I had passed. He was glad to hear the good news. I called my parents and told them the great news. We planned a celebration dinner.

Now I just had to pass the CPSE. I ordered another study packet and used a similar study plan. This time I designated six months for study time. I was able to locate a testing site for the CPSE in Sacramento, where my parents lived, so I arranged to take the test in Sacramento. That was very convenient for all of us. I was able to visit with my parents at home and take the CPSE within the same time frame. My parents did not have to come to Porterville to drive me to Fresno. My exam day was Friday morning, 6/25/10. The testing site was near my father's office and he dropped me off before going to work. After my exam, I called and my father came to take me home around his lunch time. The administrators at the testing site were very friendly and there were several other people waiting to take various exams. When my time came, I was called into the testing center and began my exam. I did not fall asleep that day. I knew I was going to pass my exam. On this day I was able to receive my exam results immediately following my exam. I was happy to receive my letter confirming that I had passed; however, the letter did not tell me my personal score. I am still curious what my score was on the CPSE, but on exam day, I was just glad to find out I had passed! I called my father, who picked me up from the exam center and I told him the great news. My family was happy for me when I told them the news. Now all I had to do was pay my initial license fee to the Board of Psychology and wait for my official psychology license! My license to practice psychology was official on 10/11/10.

Since becoming a licensed psychologist, I have received four official license cards. I have to renew my license every two years. My first license was through 6/30/12. My second license was through 6/30/14. My third license was good through 6/30/16. I recently renewed my license for the fourth time. It is good through 6/30/18. God has helped me to achieve my dream of earning my Ph.D. and earning my license to practice clinical psychology!

THE BLESSINGS
CONTINUE TO FLOW

Looking Forward to Greater Accomplishments

After earning my psychology license, I continued to provide clinical services at the state facility. A few months later, I received another unexpected blessing. One day I was checking my mailbox in the program office, when I noticed a small brown envelope. My first thought was "Oh boy. What could this be?" It did not look like anything very special or cheerful. I could not wait until I got back to my office to open it. I had to see what was inside right away so I could address it as soon as possible. While beginning my walk back to my office,

I began to read the letter inside. It was from the Executive Director, congratulating me on my nomination and win of the Superior Accomplishment Award 2010! I immediately had to share my good news with someone, so I turned around, went back inside the program office and shared the news with the program receptionist, who congratulated me. I was so happy and relieved. I could barely contain my joy. What nice news! As soon as I got back to my office, I emailed the program director, telling her the good news I received from the executive director. The program director informed me that she was the one who nominated me! I emailed her back, "Thank you!" Of course I agreed to attend the ceremony in person to receive my award! It felt nice to again be recognized and appreciated for my work.

The ceremony was scheduled for Tuesday, June 28, 2011. This just happened to be my birthday. I called my parents and told them the good news regarding my award and they visited me in Porterville on the weekend to celebrate my birthday and the award with me. We went shopping in several department stores at a local shopping center. I purchased an outfit that I thought would be nice for work and to receive my award. We went to lunch in the shopping center. We went out to dinner during the evenings. It was a fun birthday weekend for me.

Upon returning to work after the weekend, I continued to look forward to receiving the award at the ceremony. It would be held in the afternoon in the auditorium in the general treatment area. There would be many award recipients from throughout various programs on the facility campus. On the day of the ceremony, the program director was on vacation, so she designated the nursing coordinator to introduce me. He was the perfect choice. When I was initially hired, he was designated to show me around the facility, introducing me to medical staff and helping me complete my requirements to begin working. He also met my parents and was very friendly to them. He remained a friendly professional acquaintance from the time I began employment at the facility. I was glad he was the one who presented me to receive my award.

During the ceremony I received my award from the executive director himself. I was glad to meet him in person after receiving such a letter of good news from him and corresponding with him by email. He presented me with a very nice plaque. It was black with swirls of gray, kind of like a marble finish. It was 7" x 9," with an emblem at the top that read "The Great Seal of the State of California, Eureka." Below the emblem was the inscription "State of California Department of Developmental Services Superior Accomplishment Award Is presented to Elizabeth Bruce in Recognition of Your Superior Work Performance 2010."

Also present at the ceremony were a female senator of California and an assembly woman. Each presented me with awards. The Senator presented me with a certificate that read, "State of California Senate Certification of Recognition, presented to Elizabeth Bruce on behalf of the California State Senate, it is my pleasure to recognize your Exceptional Job Performance, Please accept my sincere congratulations and best wishes. Tuesday, June 28, 2011 Porterville, California, Senator 18th District." The assembly woman presented me with a certificate that read, "California State Assembly Certificate of Recognition presented to Elizabeth Bruce In honor of: Exceptional Job Performance, Dated this twenty-eighth day of June Two Thousand Eleven, Member of the Assembly, 34th Assembly District, California State Legislature. At the bottom left corner of the certificate is a golden emblem that reads "California State Assembly." That was another day of love and appreciation for me.

Counting my Blessings

The Lord has blessed me far above my wildest dreams, in such ways as helping me become a published author of an award-winning dissertation and two research articles in scholarly journals. I have also published poems with my mother and sister, collectively titled, *Poems from the Heart*, which are featured in our family cookbook, *We Remember When...* I had the honor and privilege of sharing my life testimony in my autobiography and I hope to add a fiction novel to my repertoire very soon.

Since earning my license in psychology, I have been able to purchase a home better than the one I initially tried to buy when I first moved to Porterville. I had taken a rest from searching for homes. I was not really aware of it at the time (I was simply exhausted), but I was right to wait until I obtained my license before home searching again. My qualifications improved and I was able to get a better quality home. Also, I knew the timing was right, and everything just clicked together so smoothly.

Purchasing my New Home

One day when my parents were visiting me in Porterville from Sacramento, we were all sitting at the breakfast table in my apartment dining room. Out of the blue, it came to me to say, "Would you guys like to look at new home models with me?" There was a brief silence. My mother's initial reaction was "Not at this time." Then she realized, "Oh yeah. You're going to have to be out of here soon. You better find you a place." (A few months earlier I had received a notice from the county explaining future development plans for the city and a freeway was being considered which might be going through the apartments where I was staying.) My father agreed.

We decided to begin our search on Sunday. The next day we drove to a new housing development I wanted to tour in Tulare, California, about thirty minutes from Porterville. My parents and I went inside the sales office of the housing development agency to view the models on display. There was a very friendly sales agent who gave us a tour of the models. It seemed as if God gave us immediate favor with the sales agent, because it was God's timing for me to buy a home. The sales agent kept saying to my mother, "You look very familiar. Have we met before?" My mother smiled and replied, "I don't think so." The sales agent kept insisting that she had met my mother before, but my mother could not remember.

We enjoyed viewing the models. My mother and I chose the one that we thought was best for me. It was a two story model, the second to largest. My mother and I thought the largest model would be too big. It reminded us of a famous motel that had a lobby upstairs. After our tour of the model homes, we asked the sales agent several questions regarding financing and qualifications and we took a brochure package home with us. It was a nice experience and I began seriously planning to purchase a home from the agency. The entire negotiation and purchasing process for my new home went smoothly.

One day, after consulting with my parents over the phone, I decided to apply for the purchase of the home my mother and I had chosen when we were looking at models. I called the agency and asked for the sales agent who had helped me and my parents during our visit. A man answered the phone and informed me that the sales agent I asked for was not currently available. He asked if he could help me. I informed him that I was interested in a specific model and informed him of my desired terms of purchase. The sales agent was very encouraging and helpful to me. We scheduled an appointment to meet in person and discuss options available to me for purchasing my home.

On my next visit to the sales office, I met the new sales agent who would be working with me throughout the rest of my home purchase process. He gave me another tour of the model of my prospective home and provided very helpful advice regarding finishing options for the interior design of my home. Once we were back in the office, the sales agent called the developer and did all of my negotiations for me, right there over the phone. He negotiated for me to have all of the upgrades I wanted included in my price range! I did not have to do a thing and I was able to purchase my home for less than what I had initially offered! We began the contract and I signed and initialed many papers as the sales agent explained the content to me. We made an appointment for me to bring in my initial payment to secure my purchase. That was a very nice day.

When I returned to make my initial payment, I was greeted by the sales lady who had initially given my parents and me a tour of the models. She was as pleasant as she was during our initial meeting. When I sat down with her to make my payment and review my contract, I told her who the sales agent was who helped me begin my home contract. As I explained the agreements that were negotiated, she stated, "He really got you set up didn't he?" I replied, "Yes, he sure did!" I didn't see her again after that day and negotiations were continued with the agent who began my contract with me.

During an appointment meeting, the sales agent gave me contact information and connected me with the manager of the design studio where I would be choosing finishes for the interior design of my new home. I scheduled an appointment to visit the studio in Fresno. I would be able to pick out tiles for my floors, bathroom countertops, and shower, granite countertop for my kitchen, and carpet for my entire home. It was during fall, and the weather was not foggy yet. The sun was still shining, so I knew I would be able to drive to Fresno with clear visibility. I informed my parents of my appointment at the design center in Fresno and they were happy for me.

On Monday, October 3, 2011, I took a trip to Fresno via highway 99 from Tulare. It was a beautiful sunny morning and I arrived at the design center a little early. I sat in the waiting area until my appointment time at 9AM. The manager of the design studio was very friendly. He introduced himself and guided me through the various displays in the center. He was very helpful in offering advice and suggestions for my home design. I was able to choose from a variety of beautiful options for granite, backsplash, tiles and grout, and carpet. It was fun.

After my visit to the design studio, I was given instructions to go to a granite agency to show them my choice of granite. The manager of the design studio knew I had travelled from Porterville and arranged for me to be able to go to the granite facility that day, so I would not have to make an additional road trip to Fresno. He gave me the address and directions to the granite facility and I was able to get there without difficulty. Once arriving at the granite facility, I was able to view the slab of granite that my kitchen countertops would be made from. (This courtesy was provided because granite slabs have variations in color, and the design manager wanted me to see the entire slab to be sure the color was consistent with the sample I chose at the design center.) I liked the granite color and confirmed my choice. I had a successful and fun day choosing designs for my new home. I headed back to Porterville from Fresno. It was a beautiful, peaceful, and productive day.

As my home was being built, I was able to see the progress at various phases of completion. The sales agent showed me several lot options for the location of my home that I was able to choose from. When the framing and roof were complete, the sales agent gave me a tour of my home and took a photograph of me, per my request, standing in front of my new home. Once the electrical, plumbing, and air conditioning systems were in place, the construction manager gave me a tour of the next phase of my home that was complete. I took pictures and videos of my home that day as well. When my home was almost complete, I made an appointment with the sales agent to meet me and my parents for our final tour of my home before it was finished. When we arrived, there were a few workers in my home working upstairs and we did not want to disturb them; we toured downstairs, the front yard, and the back yard. My home was coming along nicely. We went back to the office with the sales agent and discussed interest rates, the mortgage loan, and how soon I could lock in my interest at the best rate. The sales agent gave me very helpful advice. We prepared for the closing of escrow.

When it was time to sign papers with the title company, I received a call from an escrow assistant to schedule an appointment. When I informed him I would be visiting my parents out of town for a few days, he helped me arrange an appointment at my parents' home in Sacramento. That was nice and convenient and I did not have to delay my progress toward closing escrow. During my visit at my parents' home, on Friday, December 23, 2011, I signed papers with a notary for the title company. Escrow closed on December 30, 2011, and I picked up my keys, and began moving into my new home on Saturday, December 31, 2011.

The week after Christmas, my parents came to visit me in Porterville and help me move from my apartment to my new home in Tulare. We were hoping that escrow would close by Thursday, December 29, 2011, and my father would pick my keys up if they were available while I was at work, but escrow didn't close on Thursday. Even though escrow closed Friday, somehow my keys were not available until Saturday. I think it may have had something to do with the sales office hours. Scheduling was very tight during this time. My parents and I used all the time constructively. On Friday, December 30, 2011, we located a Rent-A-Center in Visalia, a city a few miles down the road from Tulare. We were able to rent a refrigerator for me to store my food until I purchased a new one of my own. We drove to Visalia and arrived at the store before closing time to schedule a delivery on Sunday, January 1, 2012.

A Busy Weekend Moving

I wanted to be out of the apartment I was renting by January 1, 2012, and I needed help moving, but I didn't have the keys to my new home yet. I would not have keys until December 31, 2011. As soon as I closed escrow, I began calling moving companies, but not many were available for New Year's Eve. Many were booked already. I was finally able to locate a moving company which was available at a reasonable price. On the morning of Saturday, December 31, 2011, I was able to greet my movers and let them help me pack and load up the moving truck. I called the sales agent and let him know that we were on our way to get my keys. Once the moving truck was loaded, the movers followed my parents and me, as my father drove, to my new address. I gave the movers my address and cell phone number in case anything unexpected occurred during the trip from Porterville to Tulare. When my parents and I arrived in Tulare, my parents took me to the sales office to get my keys, before the movers arrived. When I went inside the sales office, the sales agent congratulated me on my new home, gave me keys to my home, and gave me a very nice house warming gift basket. The basket had a dish drying towel, pasta and pasta sauce, a silver colander, cookies, and crackers. I thanked my sales agent for all of his help in the purchase of my new home. Though pleasant, the meeting felt somewhat rushed. I think it was because I had to get to my house before the movers arrived and I am sure the sales agent had prior engagements as well. After all, it was Saturday and New Year's Eve!

My parents and I arrived at my new home before the movers arrived. What a relief. We were able to open my home and have a place to move my things into! The move went smoothly. The movers placed everything where I requested. The movers complimented my home, saying it was very beautiful. I replied, "Thank you" rather enthusiastically. One of the movers who moved items into my master retreat stated, "You could play football in there!" I thought his comment was funny and I took it as a compliment. I laughed and felt happy to have my new home.

I paid the movers for their services with a personal check and said goodbye. I had a few smaller loads of items still at the old apartment and I planned to move the rest of my items by car. My parents advised me that I should have taken advantage of the movers' offer when they asked if I needed them to move the small things. I had not had time to organize and sort some smaller items the way I wanted to for moving, so I declined the movers' offer. After the movers left and after listening to my parents, I regretted declining the moving of my smaller things. I spent the entire following day moving car loads of my items to my new home from the old apartment.

My parents met me Sunday evening at the old apartment to help with final cleaning and moving out my remaining items before turning in the apartment key in the mail slot of the office at the apartment complex. Both my car and my parents' car were full of items to move, but finally it was over!

I have been in my home for four years now and I am still enjoying the newness of it. I like picking out furniture and decorative items, and interior design. Gardening and taking care of my front and back lawns is a tranquil experience for me. I helped design the landscape of my backyard and it was landscaped by professional landscapers. I have also met several friendly neighbors.

The Lord has blessed me with everything I have ever dreamed of and asked Him for. I am looking forward to fulfilling the rest of the purpose that God has created me for, which includes opening a child and family therapy clinic for the healing of children and their families. I continue to pray to God that He leads and guides me in everything I do. I know that He will continue to provide me with supernatural wisdom to represent Him with excellence in my future endeavors.

A free eBook edition is available with the purchase of this book.

To claim your free eBook edition:

1. Download the Shelfie app.
2. Write your name in upper case in the box.
3. Use the Shelfie app to submit a photo.
4. Download your eBook to any device.

Shelfie

A **free** eBook edition is available with the purchase of this print book.

CLEARLY PRINT YOUR NAME ABOVE IN UPPER CASE

Instructions to claim your free eBook edition:
1. Download the Shelfie app for Android or iOS
2. Write your name in **UPPER CASE** above
3. Use the Shelfie app to submit a photo
4. Download your eBook to any device

Print & Digital Together Forever.

Snap a photo

Free eBook

Read anywhere

Morgan James makes all of our titles available
through the Library for All Charity Organizations.

www.LibraryForAll.org

9 781683 501206